D1404565

A HOUSE
Gives Shelter

Kylie Burns
Crabtree Publishing Company
www.crabtreebooks.com

Be An Engineer!
Designing to Solve Problems

Author: Kylie Burns

Series research and development:
Janine Deschenes and Reagan Miller

Editorial director: Kathy Middleton

Editor: Petrice Custance

Proofreader: Kathy Middleton

Design and photo research: Katherine Berti

Print and production coordinator: Katherine Berti

Images:

Shutterstock
Aisyaqilumaranas: p. 13 bottom left
Pamela Brick: p. 19
s74: p. 16 bottom left
serato: p. 10

Thinkstock Photos: p. 20 (cup)

All other images by Shutterstock

Library and Archives Canada Cataloguing in Publication

Burns, Kylie, author
A house gives shelter / Kylie Burns.

(Be an engineer! Designing to solve problems)
Includes index.
Issued in print and electronic formats.
ISBN 978-0-7787-5160-1 (hardcover).--
ISBN 978-0-7787-5164-9 (softcover).--
ISBN 978-1-4271-2108-0 (HTML)

1. Dwellings--Design and construction--Juvenile literature.
2. Dwellings--Juvenile literature. 3. Structural engineering--Juvenile
literature. I. Title.

TH4811.5.B87 2018   j690'.837   C2018-902993-5
C2018-902994-3

Library of Congress Cataloging-in-Publication Data

Names: Burns, Kylie, author.
Title: A house gives shelter / Kylie Burns.
Description: New York, New York : Crabtree Publishing Company,
[2019] | Series: Be an engineer! Designing to solve problems |
Includes index.
Identifiers: LCCN 2018027893 (print) | LCCN 2018029208 (ebook) |
ISBN 9781427121080 (Electronic) |
ISBN 9780778751601 (hardcover) |
ISBN 9780778751649 (paperback)
Subjects: LCSH: Dwellings--Design and construction--Juvenile literature.
| House construction--Juvenile literature.
Classification: LCC TH4811.5 (ebook) | LCC TH4811.5 .B87 2019 (print) |
DDC 690/.8--dc23
LC record available at https://lccn.loc.gov/2018027893

Crabtree Publishing Company

www.crabtreebooks.com   1-800-387-7650

Printed in the U.S.A./092018/CG20180719

Published in Canada
Crabtree Publishing
616 Welland Ave.
St. Catharines, Ontario
L2M 5V6

Published in the United States
Crabtree Publishing
PMB 59051
350 Fifth Avenue, 59th Floor
New York, New York 10118

Published in the United Kingdom
Crabtree Publishing
Maritime House
Basin Road North, Hove
BN41 1WR

Published in Australia
Crabtree Publishing
3 Charles Street
Coburg North
VIC 3058

Contents

Hi, I'm Ava and this is Finn. Get ready for an inside look at the world of engineering! The Be an Engineer! series explores how engineers build structures to solve problems.

After reading this book, join us online at Crabtree Plus to help us solve real-world engineering challenges! Just use the Digital Code on page 23 in this book.

Safe and Sound

Alex and his family are traveling through a fishing village on the coast. A few weeks ago, many homes and businesses along the coast were destroyed in heavy **floods**. Alex knows that people who catch fish for a living must live near the ocean. He wonders if there is a way to construct buildings near water so flooding won't damage them. Alex wonders what kind of house will provide a safe shelter for people who live near the water.

Problem Solved!

Alex thought about a time when he went camping. When a rainstorm came, his tent got flooded because it was sitting on the ground. Alex began thinking about the houses on the coast. "Could there be a way to keep floodwater out?" Then he thought of the perfect solution—a house built above the ground! Being off the ground may allow water to freely pass beneath the house without damaging it.

Did you know?

All houses provide shelter, but there are many different kinds. For example, in places that flood often, houses are sometimes built on poles called stilts. Raising them off the ground solves the problem.

What Is an Engineer?

Alex is thinking about a solution to a problem. He is thinking like an engineer. An engineer is a person who uses math, science, and creative-thinking skills to **design** things to help solve problems, meet needs, and make work easier.

All Kinds of Engineers

There are many different kinds of engineers, including people who create roads, spaceships, buildings, structures, and even medicines. Not all engineers are the same. A single project, such as building a house, requires different kinds of engineers to design the structure and its materials.

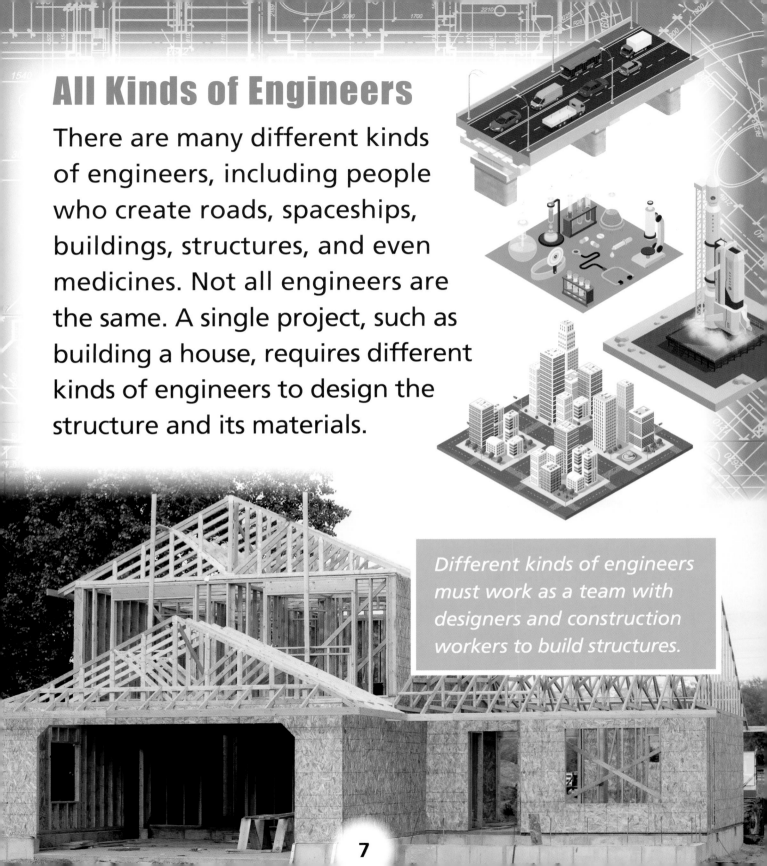

Different kinds of engineers must work as a team with designers and construction workers to build structures.

Engineers Solve Problems

Some problems are difficult to solve. Engineers follow a set of steps to solve a problem. The steps make up the Engineering Design Process. These steps can be repeated over and over until the solution is both safe and **effective**. Making mistakes is often part of this process.

1 ASK

Ask questions and gather information about the problem you are trying to solve.

2 BRAINSTORM

Work with a group to come up with different ideas to solve the problem. Choose the best solution.

The Engineering Design Process

5 COMMUNICATE

Share your design with others.

3 PLAN AND MAKE A MODEL

Create a plan to carry out your solution. Draw a diagram and gather materials. Make a **model** of your solution.

4 TEST AND IMPROVE

Test your model and record the results. Using the results, improve, or make your design better. Retest your improved design.

Asking Questions

The first step in the Engineering Design Process is to ask questions. Engineers ask questions to gather information about the problem they need to solve. If an engineer plans to build a house, it is important to find out what the **environment** is like in the area. Things such as soil, wind, water, climate, temperature, and the risk of severe weather will affect what kind of house is built.

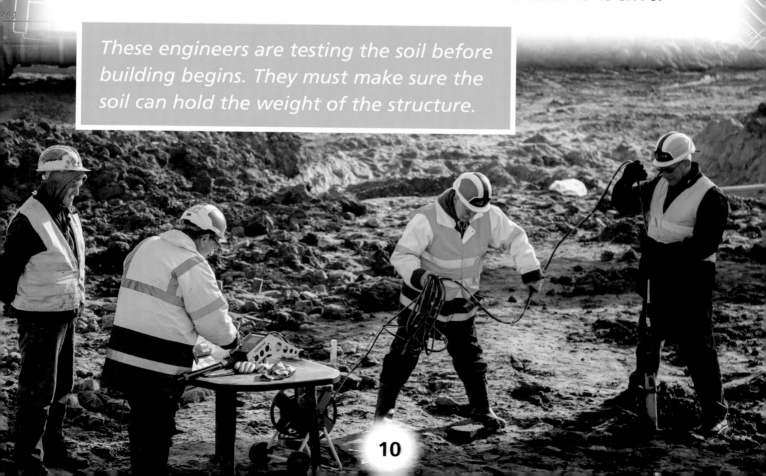

These engineers are testing the soil before building begins. They must make sure the soil can hold the weight of the structure.

Brainstorming

Once engineers have gathered their information, they brainstorm, or discuss, possible solutions to the problem with others.

A diagram like this one is useful for engineers to help them organize ideas while they are brainstorming.

Problem

Flooding is a common problem for homes and businesses in areas along the coast.

Build the homes in an area where flooding isn't common.

Use building designs and materials that can prevent floodwater from getting into homes.

Build houseboats that float on water.

Build a strong wall along the shore to hold back floodwater.

Planning

When one of the solutions is chosen, engineers begin planning. An **architect** may be part of the team that plans the building of a house. Engineers must think about the environment where the house will be built, including common weather patterns in the area. This will affect the shape of the house design, as well as which building materials the engineers choose.

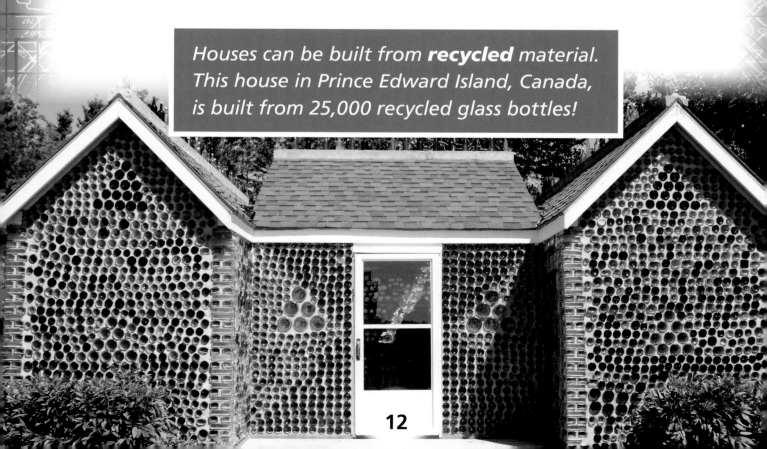

*Houses can be built from **recycled** material. This house in Prince Edward Island, Canada, is built from 25,000 recycled glass bottles!*

Engineers build sloped roofs so rainwater will flow off the building. Using materials such as concrete and tile helps keep water out.

This log home is being built using natural materials from the surrounding environment.

Engineers use clay bricks where homes need to stand up to strong winds and rain. Clay also keeps the temperature inside comfortable.

An engineer may build a home with a triangle shape so heavy snow and ice can slide off the roof easily.

Creating a Model

Once the planning stage is complete, engineers create a model of the house. A model is a smaller version of a real object. Models can be built as **3-D** objects or onscreen using computer programs. A model can be shown to builders so they can see how the finished house should look. Models are also used to test and improve the design.

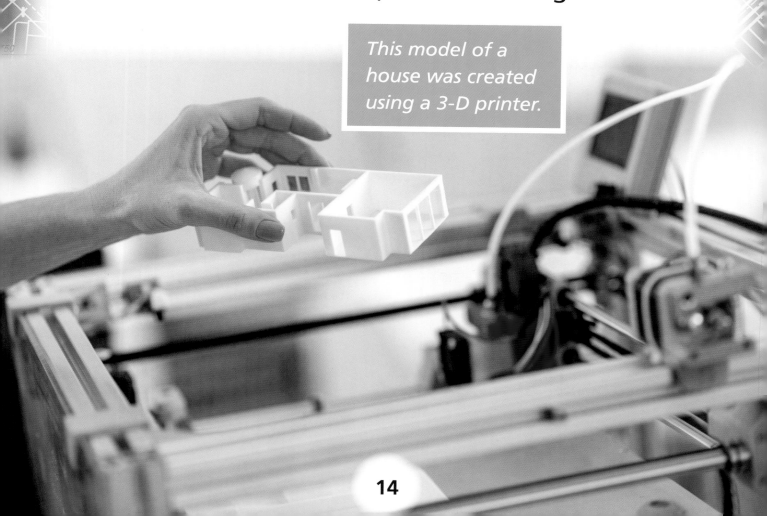

This model of a house was created using a 3-D printer.

Testing and Improving

Performing tests allows engineers to find out if parts of a design need fixing or improving. A model of a house can be tested to see if the structure will stand up to the strong shaking of an **earthquake** or the high winds of a **hurricane**. Engineers record the results, make improvements, and retest the model.

Sharing the Results

The last step in the Engineering Design Process is for engineers to share their results. This helps engineers determine which designs work, and which don't. They share results to make sure houses are built safely. Over time, sharing results has improved the design of houses, making them safer for people who live in them.

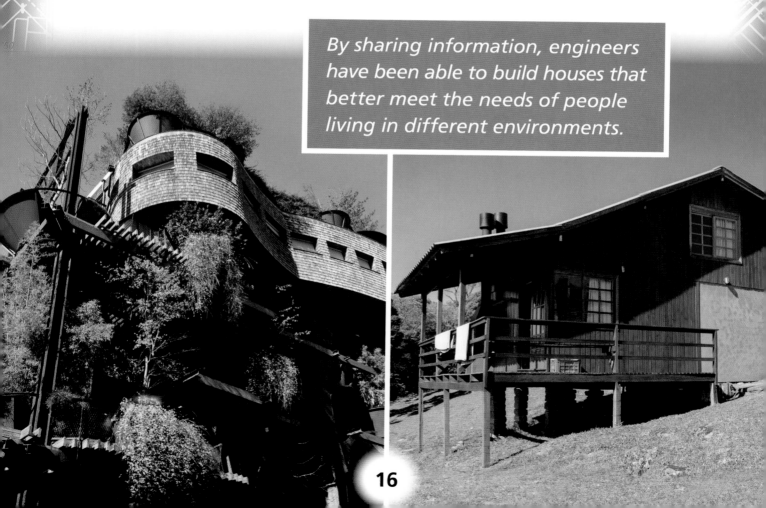

By sharing information, engineers have been able to build houses that better meet the needs of people living in different environments.

Then and Now

Houses are built to provide people with shelter. Long ago, houses were often built with materials that were easily damaged in storms or severe weather, destroying homes. Over time, technology has improved. Engineers now have many more choices for materials that will stand up to harsh weather. Engineers are always looking for the best materials to make houses strong and safe.

*Modern materials such as concrete, steel, glass, aluminum, and plastic help engineers make sure that houses resist floods, hurricanes, **tornadoes**, and earthquakes better than in the past.*

Engineers added aluminum shutters to the windows of this coastal home. Shutters provide protection to the glass during strong winds.

Step by Step

Safety is a concern for engineers when designing and building houses. It is very important that engineers closely follow each step in the Engineering Design Process. If they don't, important information may be missed, and mistakes can be made. If a mistake is made in the design of a house, people's lives might be in danger.

These engineers are closely inspecting buildings to make sure they were built safely.

Building Failure

A building failure happens when a home or other building no longer provides shelter or protection. Following Hurricane Katrina in 2005, many homes in New Orleans, Louisiana, had to be rebuilt. Some engineers did not plan well for the environment and weather. Flat roofs and poor building materials allowed moisture to get into the houses. This caused dangerous **mold** to grow in the homes.

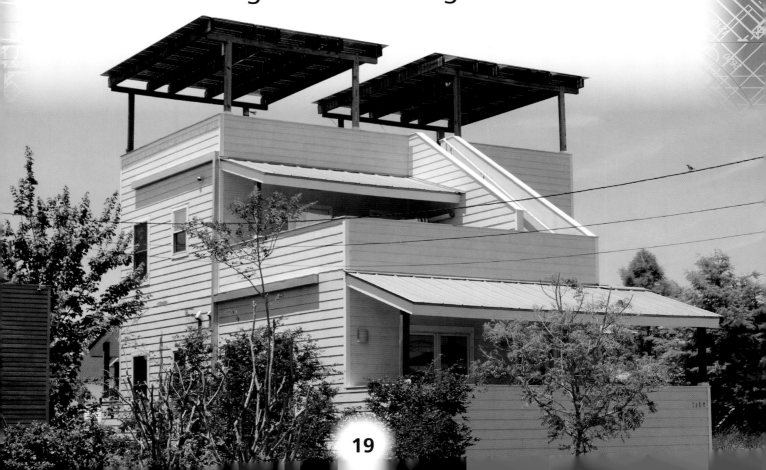

Model Activity

Using a model to test a house design is an important step in the Engineering Design Process. Testing helps engineers to make sure a house can stand up to wind, rain, floods, and earthquakes so the people who live there remain safe. Try it out for yourself by making and testing a model of a house that can stand up to wind.

You will need:

A large paper or plastic cup

2 pieces of cardstock or heavy paper

Sand

Toothpicks

Masking tape

Scissors

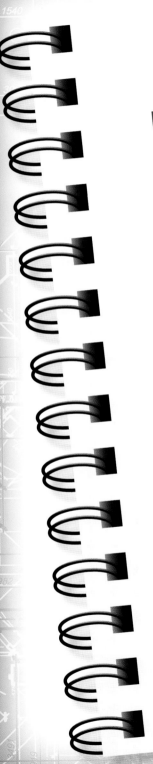

Instructions:

1. On a piece of cardstock, draw an outline of a house about 2 inches (5 cm) wide. Cut it out.
2. Fill the plastic cup to the top with sand.
3. Stand the house up on the sand in the cup.
4. Use the second piece of cardstock as a fan to blow air on the house. Observe the results. Did your house remain standing?
5. Attach toothpicks to the house with tape.
6. Put the house back on the sand, burying the toothpicks below the surface.
7. Use the cardstock again to fan the house with air.

Did your house remain standing after you added the toothpicks?

How could you make your house even more stable?

Avoiding Disaster

Disasters in the past can make people look at how things have been done and find solutions to problems. When engineers use safer building materials and new designs, it helps prevent disaster in the future. For example, homes in an area where forest fires have happened are now commonly built with **fire-resistant** materials such as concrete or brick. Engineers learn from the past, sharing ideas and developing plans to make houses safer for everyone.

Did you know?

Brick slows the spread of fire. This gives people inside the building more time to get to safety.

Learning More

Books

Engineering Close-up series. Crabtree Publishing Company, 2014.

Armstrong, Simon. *Cool Architecture: Filled with Fantastic Facts for Kids of All Ages*. Pavilion Press, 2015.

Laroche, Gilles. *If You Lived Here: Houses of the World*. Houghton Mifflin Harcourt Books for Young Readers, 2011.

Ritchie, Scott. *Look at that Building: A First Book of Structures*. Kids Can Press, 2001.

Websites

https://askdruniverse.wsu.edu/category/tem
Kids ask questions about science, and Dr. Universe gives the answers. Learn cool facts about technology, engineering, and other science-related fields.

http://pbskids.org/designsquad
On this site, you can watch, read, design, and explore many engineering activities, including building an emergency shelter.

www.kidsciencechallenge.com/#/home
This website includes videos, fun games, and a science contest.

For fun engineering challenges, activities, and more, enter the code at the Crabtree Plus website below.

www.crabtreeplus.com/be-an-engineer

Your code is:
bae04

Glossary

Note: Some boldfaced words are defined where they appear in the book.

3-D (THREE-DEE) *adjective*
Short for three-dimensional, an object that has length, width, and height

architect (AHR-ki-tekt) *noun*
A person who designs the layout of buildings

design (dih-ZAHYN) *verb*
To make plans for the look of a structure or space before it is built

earthquake (URTH-kweyk) *noun*
A series of vibrations that begin in Earth's crust

effective (ih-FEK-tiv) *adjective*
Producing the correct result

environment (en-VAHY-ern-muh-nt) *noun* The surroundings in which a person, plant, or animal lives

fire-resistant (FAHYUH-r ri-zis-TUH-nt) *adjective* A material that is designed to slow the spread of fire

flood (fluhd) *noun* Large amount of water covering what is usually dry land

hurricane (HUR-i-keyn) *noun*
A severe storm with strong winds that starts over water

model (MOD-l) *noun*
A representation of a real object

mold (mohld) *noun*
A type of fungus that grows in warm, moist conditions

recycled (ree-SAHY-kuhld) *adjective*
Describing materials that are used again for a different purpose

tornado (tawr-NEY-doh) *noun*
A destructive windstorm on land that contains a long funnel-shaped cloud

A noun is a person, place, or thing. An adjective is a word that tells you what something is like. A verb is an action word that tells you what someone or something does.

Index